Human Relations Handbook: A Guide to Influence, Inspire, and Succeed in Business & Life

Copyright © 2024 by Jacob F. Ball
All rights reserved.

Printed in the United States of America

No part of this book may be reproduced, stored in a retrieval system, or transmitted in any form or by any means (electronic, mechanical, photocopying, recording, or otherwise) without the prior written permission of the author, except for brief quotations in reviews or articles.

ISBN: 9798218563943

This book is a work of nonfiction. While the author has made every effort to ensure the accuracy of the information herein, the content is provided for informational purposes only. The author assumes no responsibility for errors or omissions or for any outcomes related to the use of this material.

Published by Jacob F. Ball
First Edition: 2025

Contents

1	Introduction	1
2	The Foundation of Success	2
3	Mastering Human Connections	3
	Begin With a Smile	4
	Remember Their Name	5
	Show Genuine Interest	6
	Listen With Purpose	7
	Speak Their Interests	8
	Elevate Their Importance	9
4	The Art of Influencing Others	10
	Start With Warmth	11
	Listen First, Speak Later	12
	Understand Their Point of View	13
	Show Empathy in Action	14
	Find Common Ground	15
	Appeal to Their Values	16
	Make It Their Idea	17
	Be Tactful, Not Confrontational	18
	Avoid Conflict, Focus on Solutions	19
	Admit Mistakes With Confidence	20
	Add Drama for Impact	21
	Create a Friendly Challenge	22

Contents

5	**Leadership Essential Principles**	23
	Lead With Positivity	24
	Motivate With Purpose	25
	Recognize & Appreciate Others	26
6	**Leading with Empathy & Impact**	27
	Begin With Genuine Praise	28
	Lead by Owning Your Mistakes	29
	Address Mistakes With Subtlety	30
	Protect Their Dignity	31
	Empower With Thoughtful Questions	32
	Guide With Encouragement & Clarity	33
	Celebrate Progress, Big or Small	34
	Inspire Enthusiasm for Your Ideas	35
	Build a Reputation They'll Aspire To	36
7	**Final Thoughts**	37

Introduction

"Be wiser than other people if you can, but do not tell them so."

- Philip Stanhope, 4th Earl of Chesterfield

Success in life and business often hinges on how well we connect with others.

This handbook encapsulates timeless human relations principles to help you excel in relationships, business, and leadership.

The Foundation of Success

85% of financial success stems from personality and the ability to communicate, negotiate, and lead.

The greatest people desire two key things:
1. To be healthy.
2. To get along with others.

This handbook will equip you with skills to connect, influence, and lead effectively.

Mastering Human Connections

Mastering Human Connections

Begin With a Smile

Happiness is a state of mind shaped by your attitude, it comes from within, not from external circumstances.

Always greet someone with a smile.

Your smile is a messenger of good will.

Mastering Human Connections
Remember Their Name

One of the most powerful things is the ability to walk into a room and use everyone's names.

Build fast associations to make names more memorable, think of a rhyming word or related noun and create a mental image connecting it to the person.

Mastering Human Connections
Show Genuine Interest

People appreciate being seen, heard, and valued.

Show genuine interest about others' experiences and perspectives and you will create a sense of connection and trust, making them naturally like you.

Mastering Human Connections

Listen With Purpose

People love talking about themselves, it makes them feel valued and understood.

Listen to others actively and attentively, ask thoughtful questions they'll enjoy answering.

People are 100X more interested in themselves than in others, focusing on them creates a connection they'll appreciate and remember.

Mastering Human Connections
Speak Their Interests

Understand their interests and **engage in topics the other person enjoys** to create positive, meaningful interactions.

Be a gentleman, be agreeable.

Mastering Human Connections
Elevate Their Importance

Show respect and **make others feel valued all the time everywhere**, <u>always in an authentic way</u>.

The urge to feel appreciated separates humans from animals. Almost everyone you meet feels superior to you in some way. Allow them to feel superior.

"In my walks, every man I meet is my superior in some way…"
- Ralph Waldo Emerson

The Art of Influencing Others

The Art of Influencing Others
Start With Warmth

Begin conversations with warmth to create a welcoming and positive atmosphere.

Approaching others with **gentleness and friendliness is far more effective** in building relationships **than aggression or force.**

A kind tone encourages collaboration and leaves a lasting impression.

The Art of Influencing Others
Listen First, Speak Later

Encourage others to share their thoughts and experiences, making them feel genuinely heard and valued.

Most people would rather talk about their accomplishments than hear you boast about yours.

"If you want enemies, excel others; if you want friends, let others excel you."
- Charles Caleb Colt

The Art of Influencing Others
Understand Their Point of View

Consider the other person's feelings and ideas as important as your own to gain cooperativeness.

Before communicating, envision why they would be motivated to do what you are asking.

Start conversations by clearly sharing the purpose and direction, while considering how you would feel as the listener.

The Art of Influencing Others
Show Empathy in Action

80% of humans crave sympathy, offer it sincerely, and they will love you.

Show genuine compassion and understanding for others' feelings and goals.

Delay sending aggressive or reactive responses for two days to gain perspective and clarity, ensuring your communication is thoughtful, constructive, and effective.

The Art of Influencing Others
Find Common Ground

Start with small agreements, get them saying yes, it increases the chances of engaging attention and gaining acceptance for your proposal.

When someone says "Yes," it creates an open, forward-moving, and accepting attitude, both mentally and physically.

When someone says "No," their entire body (nervous, muscular, and glandular) responds with a state of rejection and defensiveness.

The Art of Influencing Others
Appeal to Their Values

Appeal to others' sense of integrity and higher values.

When you align your message with their core principles and aspirations, it resonates deeply, fostering trust and motivation.

The connection with their nobler instincts empowers them to take pride in their choices and act with clarity and purpose.

The Art of Influencing Others
Make It Their Idea

Present ideas in a way that encourages the other person to take ownership and feel invested in the outcome.

<u>Do not dictate</u>, instead, make thoughtful suggestions and **guide the conversation so they arrive at the conclusion themselves.**

The Art of Influencing Others

Be Tactful, Not Confrontational

If you cannot be certain you're right more than 60% of the time, then <u>avoid telling someone they are wrong</u>.

Criticism, whether expressed through words, gestures, or looks, rarely changes minds and will cause most people to become defensive.

Teach and persuade skillfully, so others embrace new ideas without feeling forced or diminished.

"Men must be taught as if you taught them not, things unknown proposed as things forgot." - Alexander Pope

The Art of Influencing Others
Avoid Conflict, Focus on Solutions

Handle disagreements with diplomacy, avoid arguments.

Listen sincerely and fully to your opponent first before speaking, transform the conflict into an opportunity for understanding and resolution.

Disarm them by acknowledging any points where they might be right.

The Art of Influencing Others
Admit Mistakes With Confidence

Own up to your mistakes, it not only builds trust but also diffuses tension.

Humans want to feel important, when you humbly admit your shortcomings, it often prompts them to take the opposite stance and defend you.

Fighting often amplifies the problem, while yielding allows for resolution and unexpected growth.

"What you resist, persists." - Carl Jung

The Art of Influencing Others

Add Drama for Impact

Present your ideas vividly and engagingly to capture and hold attention.

Use compelling stories, relatable examples, or striking imagery **to make your points resonate** and stick.

This approach creates an emotional connection, making your message more persuasive and memorable.

The Art of Influencing Others
Create a Friendly Challenge

Human nature thrives on challenges and the pursuit of meaningful goals, as they provide a sense of purpose and fulfillment.

Present a clear objective or challenge **to activate the innate human desire for achievement** and growth, sparking motivation and **inspiring immediate action**.

"What man actually needs is a worthwhile goal." - Viktor Frankl

Leadership Essential Principles

Leadership Essential Principles
Lead With Positivity

<u>Criticism is like a boomerang; it always comes back.</u>

When you criticize or condemn someone, human nature compels them to do the same, straining the relationship.

Practice empathy and understanding, **create a positive environment that promotes** trust, collaboration, and **mutual respect**.

"Do not judge, or you too will be judged."
- Matthew 7:1

Leadership Essential Principles
Motivate With Purpose

Inspire action by arousing an eager desire in others to achieve their goals.

Focus on understanding what the other person truly wants, and clearly show how they can attain it.

Aligning their aspirations with the bigger picture creates a shared purpose that drives cooperation, builds lasting motivation, and strengthens relationships through respect for their needs and ambitions.

Leadership Essential Principles
Recognize & Appreciate Others

Humans crave recognition for their efforts and contributions, **provide genuine praise and you'll earn their heart**.

By acknowledging others strengths and achievements, you create a positive environment that encourages <u>trust</u>, <u>loyalty</u>, and <u>collaboration, essential for effective leadership</u>.

"The deepest principle in human nature is the craving to be appreciated."
- William James

Leading With Empathy & Impact

Leading With Empathy & Impact

Begin With Genuine Praise

Always start the conversation by offering sincere praise and honest appreciation to create a positive foundation for your conversation.

Beginning with positive feedback makes the other person feel valued, promoting a sense of trust and making them more open to discussing challenges or areas for improvement.

This approach is essential for effective and empathetic leadership.

Leading With Empathy & Impact

Lead by Owning Your Mistakes

Talking about your errors first softens the delivery of criticism, making it easier for the other person to accept feedback without feeling defensive.

Before offering constructive feedback, acknowledge your own mistakes to create a sense of humility and shared humanity.

This approach demonstrates vulnerability and builds trust, showing that <u>growth is a mutual process</u> rather than a one-sided judgment.

Leading With Empathy & Impact
Address Mistakes With Subtlety

Subtle, thoughtful feedback not only helps address the issue but also strengthens the relationship and promotes collaboration.

Draw attention to mistakes in an indirect and constructive manner, focusing on guidance rather than criticism.

By gently leading others to recognize their errors on their own, you preserve their dignity and encourage self-reflection.

Leading With Empathy & Impact
Protect Their Dignity

Allow the other person to save face by addressing mistakes or issues with tactfulness and respect.

Avoid actions or words that could embarrass them.

Preserving their dignity promotes trust and encourages a positive response to feedback.

Create an environment of mutual respect, where individuals feel valued and supported rather than judged.

Leading With Empathy & Impact

Empower With Thoughtful Questions

<u>Do not issue direct orders</u>, **frame your requests as thoughtful questions**.

Questions encourage others to think critically and take ownership of their actions, making them feel respected and valued.

By inviting input through questions, you inspire a sense of partnership and shared purpose, strengthening your leadership impact.

Leading With Empathy & Impact

Guide With Encouragement & Clarity

Encourage others by framing mistakes as opportunities for growth and presenting <u>solutions in clear, manageable steps</u>.

By focusing on achievable steps and expressing belief in their abilities, you empower them to overcome challenges and succeed.

"Our greatest glory is not in never falling, but in rising every time we fall."
- Confucius

Leading With Empathy & Impact

Celebrate Progress, Big or Small

Genuinely acknowledge and praise every improvement, <u>no matter how small</u>.

Recognizing progress boosts confidence and reinforces positive behaviors, creating momentum for continued development.

Small wins are stepping stones to larger successes; by celebrating them, you promote motivation, build morale, and inspire ongoing commitment to improvement.

Leading With Empathy & Impact

Inspire Enthusiasm for Your Ideas

Focus on how your ideas align with their goals or interests, highlighting the benefits and positive outcomes they will achieve.

Present your suggestions in a way that excites and motivates others, making them genuinely happy to take action.

"If you would persuade, appeal to interest rather than intellect." - Benjamin Franklin

Leading With Empathy & Impact

Build a Reputation They'll Aspire To

When you trust people with a positive and aspirational image of themselves, you inspire them to rise to the occasion and prove themselves capable.

Give others a fine reputation to live up to by setting high expectations and expressing confidence in their ability to meet them.

"Treat a man as he is, and he will remain as he is. Treat a man as he can and should be, and he will become as he can and should be." - Johann Wolfgang von Goethe

Final Thoughts

Relationships are the foundation of success, serving as the currency that fuels both personal and professional growth.

By mastering these principles, you can build stronger connections, foster trust, and create meaningful collaborations that lead to thriving in business and life.

Strong relationships not only open doors to new opportunities but also provide the support and inspiration needed to achieve your goals.

www.ingramcontent.com/pod-product-compliance
Lightning Source LLC
Chambersburg PA
CBHW071228160426
43196CB00012B/2455